UPSIDE DOWN LIVING

prayer

[The *Upside-Down Living* series emphasizes living out
one's Christian faith through the lens of Jesus,
by following values that seem so countercultural
they appear to be upside down.]

Kelly Chripczuk

HERALD
P R E S S

Harrisonburg, Virginia

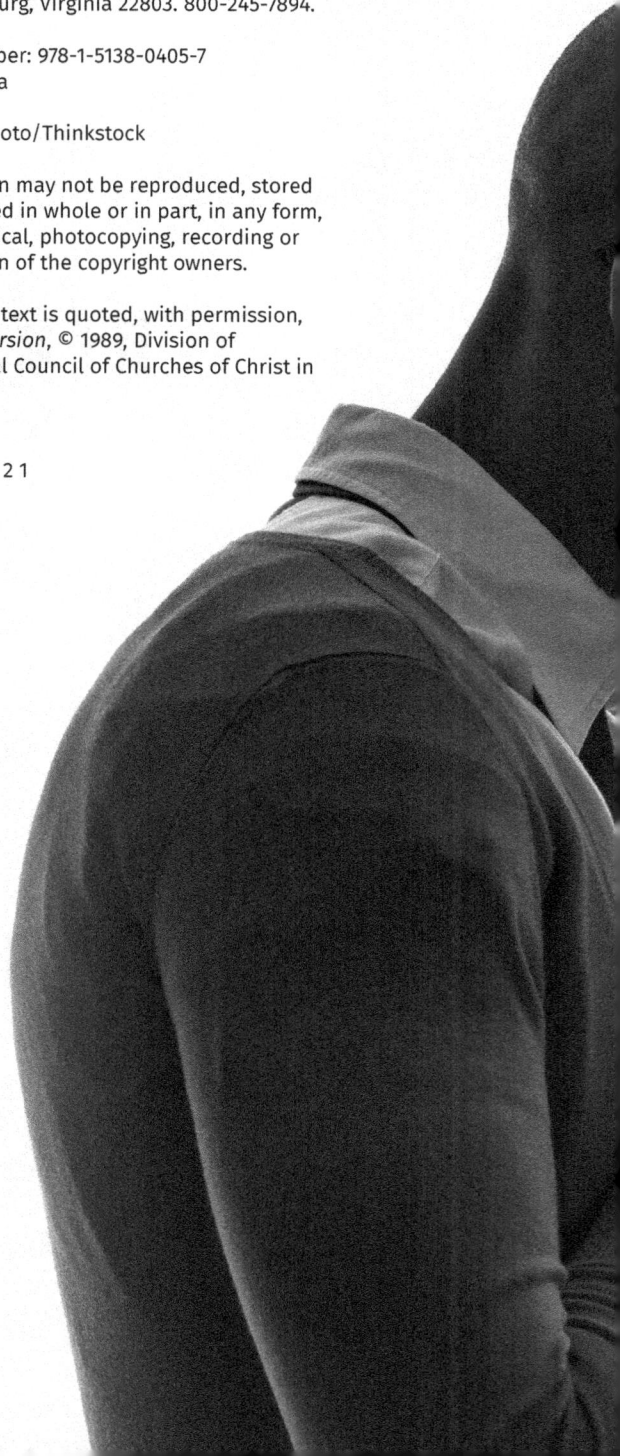

Upside-Down Living
Prayer

© 2018 by Herald Press, Harrisonburg, Virginia 22803. 800-245-7894.
   All rights reserved.
International Standard Book Number: 978-1-5138-0405-7
Printed in United States of America
Design by Merrill Miller
Cover photo by Rawpixel/iStockphoto/Thinkstock

Unless otherwise noted, Scripture text is quoted, with permission,
from the *New Revised Standard Version*, © 1989, Division of
Christian Education of the National Council of Churches of Christ in
the United States of America.

22 21 20 19 18   10 9 8 7 6 5 4 3 2 1

[Contents]

[Introduction]

Talking openly and honestly about our prayer lives can feel as taboo as talking about sexuality or finances. It's a topic we enter into with some level of fear and trepidation. Many of us worry we're doing prayer all wrong, and most of us believe we're not praying nearly enough. Our strong feelings about prayer reveal our desire. Most believers agree: we want to pray more. Somewhere, deep down, we truly long to "get it right." Yet without conversation and experimentation, how can we ever even know what "getting it right" looks or feels like?

Whether out of duty or desire, we recognize that prayer is the cornerstone of relationship with God. As a spiritual director, I agree. Many of the people I mentor want me to prescribe a prayer life for them—something like a marathon training program for athletes that starts off hard and gets harder still. I almost always refrain.

Instead, I ask them to tell me about their lives. What do they enjoy? What activities fill them with love, hope, or longing? Start your prayers there, I say. A sustainable prayer life begins with the truth of our lives, just as they are. Maybe this study will help you find a place of prayer already present in your life, just waiting to be explored.

Growing in prayer begins with talking about prayer. This six-session study will give you the opportunity to do just that. You will get the most out of these conversations if you approach them openly and honestly, listening to your own life and the lives of those in your group. What is God showing you about the state of your prayer life? What is it you desire most? What is God's good invitation to you?

Prayer is an essential guide for those who endeavor to embody the countercultural vision of Jesus' upside-down kingdom. Prayer serves as a compass, orienting us and pointing us in the direction we must go. In prayer, we yield to the gravitational pull of God and find ourselves, like the earliest disciples, equipped to turn the very world on its head.

This study—whether on your own or with a small group or Christian education class—isn't designed to answer your questions about prayer, nor does it propose a crash diet-type prayer plan that will have you praying three hours a day in six weeks or less. This study aims to broaden and deepen your understanding of prayer while presenting you with different practices to "try on for size." Some practices may surprise you with their simplicity. Hopefully all will leave you encouraged and connected as your relationship with God grows in breadth and depth.

—*Kelly Chripczuk*

PRAYER IS SPACIOUS:
One Size Doesn't Have to Fit All

My husband and I frequently text each other throughout the day. Sharing funny stories, complaints, and friendly reminders helps us stay in touch and often adds a bit of humor to our lives. Once, in the middle of a busy day at home, my phone pinged, announcing an incoming message. My husband texted:

"Felt so fat all morning. Started to feel really bad about myself. Finally, went into the bathroom and checked. Realized I am wearing your pants!"

I laughed out loud at the image of my poor, uncomfortable husband fretting over what felt like sudden weight gain. Imagine his relief when he discovered the problem

wasn't him—it was the pants! From then on, we made sure our nearly identical pants ended up in the correct drawers.

It would have been strange, if not outright bizarre, if he had continued to wear my slacks, knowing they're too small. Stranger still if he had let their fit continue to influence his perception of himself. Yet many of us do something similar when it comes to prayer. We accept a definition of prayer that's too small, to the point of discomfort. Then we allow that discomfort to foster a sense of shame and failure. Left unchecked, our sense of failure can eat away at the very heart of our relationship with God.

It's nearly impossible to find a Christian who doesn't struggle with prayer. Distraction, busyness, and the inability to find words to match our deepest desires top the list of common problems. Many people simply don't enjoy praying; for them, prayer is boring and often feels like work. Those who struggle might be relieved to know they're in good company.

> **"I was more anxious for the hour of prayer to be over than I was to remain there."**
> —Saint Teresa of Ávila

The famous Saint Teresa of Ávila said of her own prayer life, "I was more anxious for the hour of prayer to be over than I was to remain there. I don't know what heavy penance I would not have gladly undertaken rather than practice prayer."[1]

---

1   Quoted in Mark O'Keefe, Order of Saint Benedict (OSB), *The Way of Transformation: Saint Teresa of Avila on the Foundation and Fruit of Prayer* (Washington, DC: ICS Publications, 2016), 139.

Some of our struggles are because of human nature. We're "prone to wander," as one hymn puts it, burdened with limited attention spans and busy schedules of our own making. Other issues stem from a lack of clarity. Although prayer is often modeled in worship services, few churches offer interactive, experiential teaching around prayer. As a result, many adults still think of and experience prayer in the same simple terms they learned as children. Everything else in their lives has changed, grown, and expanded, but their understanding of prayer has not.

> **"Pray as you can, and don't try to pray as you can't."**
> —John Chapman

Wisdom invites us, when we find ourselves stuck and struggling, to let go of what no longer works and turn our energies toward discovering practices that truly fit the lives we live. As Catholic priest John Chapman puts it, "Pray as you can, and don't try to pray as you can't."[2]

Episcopal priest and author Barbara Brown Taylor, a self-described "failure at prayer," offers two helpful ideas when it comes to expanding our view of prayer. **First,** she suggests that "prayer is more than my idea of prayer."[3] We all have our own ideas and expectations that sometimes set a rather narrow view of the scope of prayer. What if we viewed our struggles with prayer not as a sign of failure, but as a sign that our concept of prayer is, ill-fitted to our temperament, too small or out of sync with our current stage of life? Acknowledging the spacious nature of prayer awakens us to the hopeful possibility of finding a better fit.

---

2   John Chapman, OSB, *Spiritual Letters* (New York: Burn and Oates, 1935), 61.
3   Barbara Brown Taylor, *An Altar in the World: A Geography of Faith* (New York: Harper Collins, 2009), 176.

What if prayer is simply a way of describing the ways we're in relationship with God? Prayer is not defined by what we do or say but by our awareness of God's presence. To pray is to practice continually opening ourselves to that presence. Such a spacious definition reveals there's no arena of life in which we cannot potentially encounter God. The variety of ways of being with God are, in truth, endless. We might sit quietly with God, marveling at the simple grace of birds visiting a feeder outside the kitchen window. Or we might cry or laugh with God about the joys and struggles of life. Sometimes we may even argue with God, before perceived distance gives way to a new depth of relatedness. Prayer is less about what we do or say and more about recognizing who we are with.

Taylor's second insight is that some of what she already does may count as prayer. This is lovely news for everyone frustrated, ashamed, or discouraged about their prayer life. Humans are created for meaningful relationship with God, and the incarnation of Jesus reveals God's natural inclination toward humanity. With the longing love of God pursuing us, is it any wonder that our hearts sometimes make their way toward God without us even knowing it?

> Isn't it possible that the opening and lifting of one's heart toward what is unseen might be called prayer?

Take, for example, the hope, joy, and gratitude a gardener feels in tilling the earth and sowing seed. Isn't it possible that the opening and lifting of one's heart toward what is unseen might be called prayer? Or think of the trust and surrender embodied in our nightly rest or a necessary afternoon nap. Might not this also be called prayer?

Some years ago, while parenting four young children, I had little time for solitary, focused prayers. What I *did* have were mountains of laundry. Every day, I washed, folded, and sorted onesies, sleepers, and socks. When a dear friend asked me how I prayed for my children, I thought for a moment. "When I'm doing laundry, I feel my love for my children rise in my chest," I said. "Does this count as prayer?"

My wise friend said, "Yes, that counts!" I found myself encouraged by the discovery of a way of prayer that fit my laundry-filled life just right.

The idea that we may already be praying more than we realize is not an excuse to pray less. Rather, it is an invitation to take heart and pay attention. God's desire is to be with us. God is, in fact, already with us, always. A spacious life of prayer is one in which we open wide our hearts and choose to be aware of the presence of God in all we do and say.

Talk about it

▶ Spend a few minutes thinking about your experiences with prayer. How did you pray as a child? Who taught you to pray? Has your prayer life changed as your life and faith have grown and shifted?

▶ Do you struggle to pray? If so, why?

▶ "Prayer is . . ." activity: Find a blank sheet of paper. Set aside five to seven minutes to come up with as many ways as you can to finish the sentence "Prayer is . . ." Try not to pause too long between sentences, and keep writing until time runs out. Share your answers with your group. Listen for similarities and differences in your lists. Are there any answers that surprise you?

▶ Are there any activities in your life that feel like prayer to you? Try to think of two or three activities during which the feelings and thoughts you associate with prayer are present. Is there a one-sentence prayer you might say before, during, or after these activities to acknowledge your awareness of God's presence in them?

2 PRAYER IS LISTENING:
[Tending Your Core]

I once spent several months in physical therapy to address lower back pain. Near the beginning of treatment, I lay flat on my back on a cushioned table with knees bent, lifting my body in and out of bridge pose. "How does that feel?" the therapist asked.

"I feel it pull a little in my lower back," I said.

"Are you using your core?" he asked.

I paused, listened to my body, and got no reply. "What do you mean?" I asked.

"You want to be using your abdominal muscles to lift," he said. "It's all about relearning to use those muscles."

I tried tightening my lower stomach. "Hello," my abdominal muscles whispered, as if waking from a long nap. The therapist explained that the lower abdominal muscles, commonly referred

> [**I wondered: how had I spent years of my life completely disengaged from my core?**]

to as the core, act as a natural girdle, keeping the pelvis and spine in alignment. As I continued to exercise, I wondered: how had I spent years of my life completely disengaged from my core?

I had developed the habit of using my body without really paying attention to *how* I was using it. Focused on getting the groceries put away or the laundry basket up the stairs, I didn't realize I was hurting myself in the process. Only when my muscles spasmed did I stop and admit something was wrong. Health required relearning how to listen to my body and adjusting my actions according to what I heard.

Prayer is the core of our spiritual lives. Like those all-important transabdominal muscles, prayer keeps us properly aligned with God, self, and others. Its neglect can lead to disastrous results. Christians are some of the most active people I know. We work, raise kids, tend loved ones, lead worship, sit on committees, take meals to families with new babies, and volunteer in a dozen different ways. Often, these activities are direct extensions of our deepest beliefs. We aren't just busy; we're busy doing good things.

The more active we are, though, the more life's demands seem to multiply. As the laws of physics predict, an object in motion tends to stay in motion.

The more active we are, the more likely we are to become out of alignment with God, self, and others. The common term for this state is *burnout*: a sense of spiritual, emotional, and physical depletion. Burnout is a direct result of overactivity and long-term strain. Burnout can lead to relational discord, addictive coping behaviors, and distance in our relationship with God.

Mary's and Martha's interactions with Jesus at their home in Bethany offer an illuminating portrayal of the nature of burnout and its cure. Generous Martha invited Jesus into her home and was soon overwhelmed by the demands of hospitality.

> [Martha's accusation, "Lord, do you not care?"
> only thinly masked the depth of her pain.]

The strain quickly pulled her out of alignment. Seeking relief from the pain of perceived abandonment, Martha chastised her sister and pulled Jesus into the dispute. Her accusation, "Lord, do you not care?" only thinly masked the depth of her pain.

Jesus, however, identified the real issue behind Martha's demanding words. Rather than judging or condemning, Jesus said her name twice, effectively calling her home to himself. Then he identified the reality of her situation: "Martha, Martha, you are worried and distracted by many things" (Luke 10:41).

Jesus' diagnosis of Martha's condition rings true for many modern believers. Stretched thin, we find ourselves close to choices that cause real and lasting spiritual, relational, and personal harm. If worry and distraction are the diagnosis, then learning to listen again and adjust our movements to what we hear is the cure. Jesus' invitation to Martha—to draw near and tend, first, to the core—extends to us too.

Many Christians warily accept—or perhaps secretly resist—this passage, because Jesus' comment that "there is need of only one thing" offers a direct challenge to our sense of urgency. Sitting at Jesus' feet when there's clear work to be done feels impractical at best. But dismissing Jesus' invitation as impractical fails to honor the depth of Martha's pain and the depth of compassion embodied in Jesus' response. Like the father's hope in the parable of the prodigal son, Jesus' deepest desire is for Martha to be aligned with him. Everything else comes second.

Many of us experience prayer as yet another extension of our already busy, noisy lives. We fill prayer with words upon words upon more words. When words run out, we're done for the day and move on to the next task at hand. If we're going to survive and thrive in our busy lives, we need prayer practices that allow us to "sit at Jesus' feet," where we learn to recognize and respond to God's voice.

Listening prayer directly contradicts our tendency
to play God by forcing us to look beyond the rise and fall of our busy lives and listen for the "still, small voice of God." Listening prayer recognizes the otherness of God, restoring our awareness of God as the only one capable of offering balance, direction, and nourishment for our active lives. In the language of theologian Paul Tillich, we recognize God as our "Ground of Being." God is the good and fertile soil in which we're invited to grow deep roots.

Lectio divina, or divine reading, is one of the simplest and most popular forms of listening prayer. *Lectio,* as it's commonly called, puts aside intellectual study of Scripture in favor of prayerful attention as we listen for God's word *to us.* Rather than having us skim substantial portions of Scripture, *lectio* invites us to read a short passage slowly and attentively, similar to the way an athlete might carefully practice a difficult maneuver. Slowed and stilled, we listen deeply for God's voice. Listening, we learn to hear.

Although practices may vary slightly, *lectio* involves reading a passage four times, incorporating the following steps:

1. **Read:** Read slowly and reflectively, listening for any word or phrase that draws you.

2. **Reflect:** Read the passage again, continuing to listen. What is the shape of God's word to you?

3. **Respond:** Read a third time, then spend time journaling your response. Think of this as a conversation with Jesus.

4. **Rest:** Read one last time, then sit silently, resting at Jesus' feet and trusting in God's work in you.

Through time devoted to learning Jesus' voice, much like my own therapy aimed at learning to listen to my muscles, many people find that a posture of listening can become a way of life. We can begin to allow the movements of listening and aligning to become intuitively woven into the fabric of our days. This approach to prayer is a source of great joy and strength. In each moment Jesus continues to invite us, by name, to make our home at his feet. Indeed, there is need of only one thing. From it all else flows.

Talk about it

▶ Reflect on the image of prayer as a realigning practice. Does this resonate for you? Do you prioritize listening in prayer, or do you tend toward more active expressions?

▶ What things cause your life to feel out of alignment? What impact does an overactive life have on your spirit and relationships?

▶ Many people have a strong reaction to the story of Jesus' visit with Mary and Martha. What feelings does the story arouse in you? Do you relate to Martha's behaviors? Does Jesus' diagnosis of Martha as being "worried and distracted" ring true for you?

▶ How do you respond to Jesus' words "There is need of only one thing"? Does his response to Martha seem practical? Does it matter whether it's practical?

▶ Try practicing *lectio divina* with the Luke 10:38-42 passage. Check out this free, downloadable introduction from the FOCUS blog: https://focusoncampus.org/content/how-to-pray-lectio-3-easy-steps

3 PRAYER IS VULNERABLE:
A Path to Intimacy and Belonging

Several years into parenting, I noticed that our bedtime prayers with our children were woefully lacking. I longed to send my kids to sleep with compelling images of a loving God and reminders that we are coworkers in the kingdom of God. But putting together a prayer like that is a tall order, even on the best of days. Admitting my limitations, I gathered and printed out prayers from traditional prayer books and hung a copy in each child's room.

Prayers like this, from *The Book of Common Prayer*, added the missing breadth and depth I sought:

> Keep watch, dear Lord, with those who work, or watch, or weep this night, and give your angels charge over those who sleep. Tend the sick, Lord Christ; give rest to the weary, bless the dying, soothe the suffering, pity the afflicted, shield the joyous; and all for your love's sake. *Amen.*[1]

---

1   *The Book of Common Prayer* (New York: Seabury Press, 1979), 124.

But they also stirred up a vague discomfort in me that went un-named until I read this statement by Mahatma Gandhi: "Prayer . . . is daily admission of one's weakness."[2]

Gandhi helped me see that my dis-ease stemmed directly from the prayers' breadth and depth. Interceding for the sick, the dying, the suffering, and the afflicted: well, it left me feeling weak. Praying for situations whose solutions lay beyond my grasp highlighted my limitations, and addressing the sorrow of human-ity made my own humanity uncomfortably clear. Our bedtime prayers became admissions of weakness and vulnerability, and I was uncomfortable with that.

Prayer's vulnerability can leave even the bravest among us stut-tering and stammering. Even the liveliest Bible study can descend into awkward silence when the time for sharing prayer requests ar-rives. Someone may share the health concerns of a distant relative

[Seldom do we name the things we struggle with most.]

or ask for "traveling mercies" for an upcoming trip. But seldom do we name the things we struggle with most. What's more, it's rare for such groups to sit in prayerful humility, acknowledging the enormity of the greater world's unmet needs. Such prayers leave us painfully aware of our insufficiency and of the grief and trag-edy we long to ignore.

Beyond interpersonal vulnerability, however, prayer invites vul-nerability with God. Prayer is vulnerable by nature. To pray is to

---

2   Quoted in Richard Attenborough, comp., *The Words of Gandhi*, 2nd ed. (New York: Newmarket Press, 2008), 64.

ask, to request, to name a need. If we hesitate to name need in community, then we're also likely hesitant to name need in our own private conversations with God. Perhaps we believe we need to fix areas of our lives before we allow God to "go there." So we hide our true needs, even in prayer. Hiding real need can result in

> [The deepest, most fruitful relationships
> are built on measured risk and trust.]

pious, passionless prayers (like the Pharisee in Jesus' story, which we'll look at soon). Or we may stop praying altogether. Here the old proverb "Nothing ventured, nothing gained" applies. The deepest, most fruitful relationships are built on measured risk and trust.

Jesus' parable in Luke 18:10-14 addresses the practice of offering prayers that reveal little, if any, of the heart's true condition:

> Two men went up to the temple to pray, one a Pharisee and the other a tax collector. The Pharisee, standing by himself, was praying thus, "God, I thank you that I am not like other people: thieves, rogues, adulterers, or even like this tax collector. I fast twice a week; I give a tenth of all my income." But the tax collector, standing far off, would not even look up to heaven, but was beating his breast and saying, "God, be merciful to me, a sinner!" I tell you, this man went down to his home justified rather than the other; for all who exalt themselves will be humbled, but all who humble themselves will be exalted.

The Pharisee's prayer focused solely on his perceived strengths, while the tax collector's prayer emphasized his weakness and need for God. Jesus highlights the difference between these two prayers as being one of positioning: the Pharisee exalted himself, while the tax collector humbled himself.

Biblical humility positions us near to the heart of God.

(See Psalms 34:18; 138:6; Philippians 2:8, which note humility as a key attribute valued by God and a characteristic of Jesus himself.) Humility doesn't require the denigration or condemnation of the self but invites us to dwell in an accurate appraisal of the human condition. The English word *humility* has its origins in the Latin root *humus*, meaning "earth." Humble prayers are prayers rooted in the earthy truth of who we are, warts and all. In a culture focused on glossy self-images, such prayers are vulnerable and countercultural.

> **"Vulnerability is the birthplace of love, belonging, joy, courage, empathy, and creativity. . ."**
> —Brené Brown

Research shows that our places of perceived weakness are the very places where deep transformations are most likely to occur. Research professor Brené Brown, who studies vulnerability and shame, puts it this way: "Vulnerability is the birthplace of love, belonging, joy, courage, empathy, and creativity. It is the source of hope, empathy, accountability, and authenticity. If we want greater clarity in our purpose or deeper and more meaningful spiritual lives, vulnerability is the path."[3]

---

3   Brené Brown, *Daring Greatly: How the Courage to be Vulnerable Changes the Way We Live, Love, Parent, and Lead* (New York: Gotham Books, 2012), 34.

Vulnerable prayers acknowledge the distance between us and God, and between us and others. Then they position us to be drawn closer. Intimacy with God and others depends on our willingness to admit weakness.

How can churches begin to encourage vulnerability in prayer?
The Psalms offer a good starting point, as they model giving voice to the breadth and depth of human experience—from praise to frustration, from fear to longing and hope. Reading and praying psalms both privately and in community has a long history. It may also be helpful to offer individuals and groups less intimidating ways to share and express their deepest prayers. Opportunities to write anonymous requests or to share needs in other nonverbal ways often help people dig deeper.

Vulnerability lies at the heart of community.
Yet as with many of our most valuable assets, it's also susceptible to abuse. Deepening vulnerability also requires careful evaluation of the current shape of our communities. Are they safe places for the sharing of real concerns? Do we offer time and space for people to examine and name deeper concerns? Perhaps most importantly, how do we treat the vulnerable in our midst? Are they separated out or subtly shamed for their needs, or do we respond with compassion and allow their vulnerability to awaken our deepest humanity?

These are tough questions, not easily or lightly answered. But answering them well and honestly positions us to move beyond the surface of our lives. By owning and admitting weakness, we draw closer to the life-giving, life-transforming strength of God.

Talk about it

▶ How do you respond to the idea of prayer being an admission of weakness?

▶ How comfortable are you admitting weakness to other people? To God?

▶ Think about your prayer life. Can you name one time and place when you were encouraged to be vulnerable in prayer and one time and place when it was discouraged? How did these experiences differ? Which was more transformative for you?

▶ Can you relate to the feeling that your prayers are sometimes empty or just skimming the surface? What would it look like to increase the level of risk or vulnerability in your prayers?

▶ The tax collector's humble prayer is the basis for the Jesus Prayer: "Lord Jesus Christ, Son of God, have mercy on me, a sinner." This prayer is used by Christians all over the world as a way to reposition themselves spiritually and emotionally near to the heart of God. What impact might the repetition of the Jesus Prayer have on your life?

4 PRAYER IS IMAGINATIVE:
[Praying the Ignatian Way]

Mark's gospel tells the story of Jesus' encounter with Bartimaeus, a blind beggar who sat along the side of the road outside of Jericho. Familiar with Jesus' reputation as a healer, Bartimaeus saw an opportunity when Jesus passed by with a crowd. The blind man, it seems, envisioned another way of life for himself. Emboldened by this vision, Bartimaeus cried out for mercy. Jesus healed him on the spot. (See Mark 10:46-52 for this story.)

Many call Bartimaeus's vision faith, but I wonder if it might not also be called imagination. The word *imagination* comes from the Latin verb *imaginari*, which means "to picture oneself." Imagination is the ability to form ideas and images of things that are not present realities. An imaginative child might look at a pile of old lumber and see a tree fort, complete with turrets and moat. An imaginative cook might look in the refrigerator and picture a tasty meal pulled together from disparate ingredients. Both situations invite the ability to see what is and lean into what is not yet.

Faith, the Bible tells us, involves a very similar capacity: "Faith is the assurance of things hoped for, the conviction of things not seen" (Hebrews 11:1). If imagination is akin to faith, it's worth asking what role it might play in cultivating a powerful and vibrant prayer life.

Asking Jesus for healing required at least a spark of imagination. The lame imagined the ability to walk again, legs straight, feet pressed firmly on solid ground. Lepers imagined a return to life in community, no longer being outcasts. People of faith came to

> [Contact with Jesus kindled their ability to envision a new way of life.]

Jesus and found their imaginations enlivened by the encounter. Contact with Jesus kindled their ability to envision a new way of life. This ability became an identifying marker of Jesus' earliest followers, and later, the church.

Unfortunately, many Christians view imagination as a childish luxury or, worse, as a doorway for evil. But if we can only imagine 101 negative answers to the question "What if?" the problem isn't our imagination; it's the direction we've pointed it in. The problem with imagination, and the reason it's often viewed with suspicion, is the regularity with which we steer it

down negative or hedonistic paths. It is indeed possible to allow the imagination to be shaped by fear and greed. The human imagination, like every other aspect of our humanity, needs to be trained in holiness if it's to serve us well.

If the church is called to be the imagination of the world—the link between that which is seen and unseen—we

need prayer practices that rekindle the flames of our imaginations. Saint Ignatius of Loyola introduced the practice of imaginative prayer in a collection of meditations that came to be known as *The Spiritual Exercises*. Born in 1491 in northern Spain, Ignatius spent years of his life seeking fame and fortune before experiencing a profound conversion during a prolonged illness. Confined to his bed, Ignatius trained his vivid imagination on the gospel stories of Jesus. Hours spent in meditation led him to a life-giving encounter with Christ. Ignatius followed the path of his imagination, turning away from the life in front of him to become an influential church leader and the founder of the Jesuits.

> Through imaginative encounter, we become the kind of people who know, deep in our bones, the hands, face, and voice of Jesus.

According to Ignatius, the aim of imaginative prayer is a direct experience of God's loving presence and the kindling of our desire to know and follow Jesus. Using senses and emotions, participants move beyond ideas *about* God to experience *of* God. Through imaginative encounter, we become the kind of people who know, deep in our bones, the hands, face, and voice of Jesus. Such an encounter with Jesus multiplies faith and transforms us into the kind of people who, like Bartimaeus, "can see again."

Imaginative prayer can center on any brief gospel account in which Jesus is present. The story of Bartimaeus in Mark 10:46-52 would work well. After an initial reading, participants enter a period of prayerful participation in the gospel event. Ignatius encourages us to take the role of someone in the story: maybe Bartimaeus, a disciple, or a member of the crowd. We then use all our senses to imagine the scene before us. What sounds do we hear? How does the road feel beneath our feet? Is the air around us cool, or humid, or scented with dung?

After setting the scene, we move slowly and prayerfully through the story, observing the action and our responses to it. Imagine Jesus' face, the faces of the disciples. Listen to Jesus as he addresses the blind man. What do we notice about his voice, the way he tilts his head or reaches out a hand?

Then, after we have dwelled for some time in the passage, we complete the encounter, resting quietly or journaling about the experience.

> Encountering Christ through the use of holy imagination deepens faith and exercises our capacity to live out the already-but-not-yet dream of God's kingdom.

While imaginative prayer focuses on personal experience, its application and implications are wide reaching. Encountering Christ through the use of holy imagination deepens faith and exercises our capacity to live out the already-but-not-yet dream of God's kingdom. Cultivation of imagination is cultivation of faith in the reality that God's transformative power can permeate all of life—the human heart, mind, body, and the very world in which we live. In a world so often polarized and stuck with no clear way forward, a church filled with holy imagination may be one of the best gifts we have to offer.

Talk about it

▶ Spend a few minutes considering the role of imagination in your life. Are you an imaginative person? Were you an imaginative child? Remember, imagination can take many forms—from writing and drawing to daydreaming, doodling, or telling jokes.

▶ What reservations do you have about using your imagination in prayer?

▶ Imaginative people sometimes stick out from the crowd in awkward or unsettling ways. Jesus was like that. Have you ever been shamed for "thinking outside the box"—or for not being imaginative enough? Invite God's presence in as you reflect on your memories. What difference does Christ's presence make as you explore your imagination?

▶ Can you relate to feeling a lack of imagination in prayer? How might a more direct experience of Jesus affect your prayer life?

▶ Try practicing imaginative prayer with the Mark 10 passage about Bartimaeus. You can do this in a group or privately. Some people like to sit quietly and imagine, while others find it easier to focus by writing about the experience. If you're unsure where to begin, try using a downloadable guide from Pray as You Go: https://pray-as-you-go.org/prayer-resources/imaginative-contemplation/.

5 PRAYER IS LIFE AFFIRMING:
Breathing Blessings

I was three steps from our back door when I heard my kids calling from the middle of the yard. "Mom! Mom! Come here!"

I turned away from the warm house and trudged through heavy, wet snow. In the middle of the yard, two of my sons worked together, shoveling snow into an enormous heap.

"Do you see our pile?" they asked.

"Yeah, wow!" I said, impressed by its size.

"We're going to add on a couple more feet and turn it into a fort," they said.

"Wow," I repeated, "that's a lot of work. Good job, guys!"

Revived and affirmed, they returned to work. Walking back to the house, I thought about their desire for me to see and bless their work—which meant, by extension, seeing and blessing them. Children hunger for blessing, and the rest of us do too.

In his book *Life of the Beloved*, Catholic priest and spiritual teacher Henri Nouwen tells the story of a woman with disabilities in his community who asked for a blessing. Giving it little thought, Nouwen made a quick sign of the cross on her forehead. But she refused his simple act, saying, "I want a real blessing!" Recognizing her genuine need, Nouwen promised to offer a blessing at the end of their worship service.

When the time came, the woman rushed to the front of the chapel where Nouwen stood, and she wrapped her arms around him. Instinctively, Nouwen returned the hug, enfolding her in the

[Criticism, ridicule, or even simple dismissal are easy alternatives to the vulnerability that is required to give and receive blessings.]

long arms of his priest's robe while speaking words of affirmation and love. When he finished, she looked up and smiled. One after another, others in the room also came forward to be blessed. Nouwen was deeply touched by the experience and saw it as proof of the human desire to give and receive blessings.[1]

The language of cursing and condemnation is more common in today's popular culture than the language of blessing. Criticism, ridicule, or even simple dismissal are easy alternatives to the vulnerability that is required to give and receive blessings. Whether online or in person, many people choose condemnation instead of grace. In some church circles, the ability to condemn is even seen as a sign of holiness.

---

1   Henri J. M. Nouwen, *Life of the Beloved: Spiritual Living in a Secular World* (New York: Crossroad, 1992), 69–72.

Yet nothing could be further from the way of Jesus Christ, who came into the world not to condemn the world but to save it (John 3:17). Contrary to the Pharisees of his time, who were hyper-focused on condemning sin, Jesus stood out because of his willingness to bless the good in people, freeing and welcoming them into lives of deeper blessing.

To bless, according to Episcopal priest Barbara Brown Taylor, is to "see [a] thing for what it is and pronounce it good."[2] In this way, all blessings echo God's original blessing spoken over creation in Genesis 1: "God saw that it was good." Genesis introduces a God who blesses and a creation that's blessed. The entire Genesis account reverberates with God seeing things as they are and affirming their goodness. The Hebrew word for "good" used in Genesis doesn't denote moral qualities; instead, it refers to the

> The desire to be seen as we are and to be called "good" dwells deep within the heart of every human.

overall purposefulness and delightfulness of creation. Biblical scholar Walter Brueggemann concludes, "All of creation is characterized by God's delight . . . delight is . . . structured into the character of reality."[3]

If God's first words spoken over the whole of the created world were ones of blessing, it's no wonder we crave it still. The desire to be seen as we are and to be called "good" dwells deep within the heart of every human. Nouwen understood prayer

2   Barbara Brown Taylor, *An Altar in the World: A Geography of Faith* (New York: Harper Collins, 2009), 199.
3   Walter Brueggemann, *Genesis*, Interpretation: A Commentary for Teaching and Preaching 27 (Louisville, KY: Westminster John Knox Press), 36–38.

itself as a time of resting in this original blessing. According to Nouwen, to pray is to "listen to the voice that says good things about me."[4] Teacher and author Anthony de Mello similarly invites us to "behold the One beholding you, and smiling."[5] Many spiritual teachers suggest spending time every day resting in an awareness of God's love and blessing. Such prayer leaves us revived, affirmed, and centered in the face of the world's many competing demands.

But blessings aren't only for receiving. Shortly after

the creation account in Genesis, God sets apart a people who are blessed to be a blessing (Genesis 12:2). The path of prayer that begins with listening to the blessing transforms those who walk it into people who bless—people who see and call forth the goodness of others.

[**Imagine how attractive it would be if Christians became known again as people who bless.**]

The ancient Celtic church models Jesus' posture of blessing perhaps more clearly than any other stream of Christianity. In the Celtic tradition, blessings were prayed, spoken, and sung over nearly every activity of daily life. Blessings were bestowed upon people, animals, and even inanimate objects. There were blessings for the churning of butter, the sowing of seeds, and the birthing of children. Each of these acknowledged and invited the presence of God into every sphere of life. They didn't seek to confer holiness but recognized and affirmed it.

---

4   Nouwen, *Life of the Beloved*, 75–76.
5   Gregory Boyle, *Tattoos on the Heart: The Power of Boundless Compassion* (New York: Free Press, 2010), 20.

As blessed people, we too can become a blessing.

Imagine how attractive it would be if Christians became known again as people who bless.

My kids once took a jar of bedraggled crickets to a Blessing of the Animals service at a park near our house. The crickets weren't beloved pets—they were literally a dime a dozen—but they did fill the dark alley between our apartment and the next with song. The priest blessed them with a sprinkle of holy water and a simple prayer. We carted them back home and let them go, affirmed in our belief that even the smallest creatures exist to bless and be blessed.

Talk about it

▶ When have you been blessed, either formally or informally? What did that look like? In what ways has that blessing stayed with you?

▶ What kind of formal and informal blessings do you or your church community practice?

▶ Where do you notice the prevalence of blessing or cursing in modern culture? What influence does that have on you or on those you love?

▶ Spend some time thinking about the words *blessing*, *goodness*, and *delight*. Prayerfully imagine God calling you "good" or "delightful." Journal what thoughts come to mind as you reflect on God's delight in you. Share with the group, if you want.

▶ Why do you think Christians have moved away from the practice of speaking blessings? What's lost when we abandon the practice of blessing?

▶ Spend time listing activities you do every day. Look over the list. Are there any places where you could easily and meaningfully incorporate blessing into your day? Maybe a simple word as your children leave for school, or as you wash your hands or put on your shoes each morning?

XI XIN XING/ISTOCKPHOTO/THINKSTOCK

6 PRAYER IS ACTIVE:
[Meditation and Action Go Hand in Hand]

I was scheduled to teach a college class on the topic of meditation two days after one of the deadliest school shootings in U.S. history. As a parent of school-age children, I was rattled, and I imagined my students were, too. As we sat in the classroom that morning, one ear to the news and one eye on the door, I worried that the topic of the class period would seem irrelevant. What could meditation possibly have to do with responding to the crisis at hand?

I decided to set aside our usual opening moments of silent prayer in favor of conversation around the recent shootings and gun violence in general. Several students lamented the abundance of violence in our culture and the threat of increased desensitization. Another student was frustrated by the polarization of opinions and the lack of a clear, persuasive path toward resolution. A third student bemoaned the complexity of the issue. "How do we decide where to focus our energy?" she asked. "How do we figure out what part is ours to do?"

> Every issue requires imaginative vision capable of identifying and communicating a clear path forward.

Although we were focused on the topic of gun violence, my students' questions apply to a host of other tragedies and injustices. Every issue of social justice requires a baseline sensitivity to the wrongs of our world. Every issue requires imaginative vision capable of identifying and communicating a clear path forward. Every issue is complicated. Each of these realities can lead to indecision, polarization, and paralysis. These questions often become a stumbling block that impedes life-giving action.

Listening to my students, I was surprised to realize that meditation—that is, time spent dwelling in the presence of God—offers a means of addressing each of their questions. Far from being irrelevant, meditation offers fertile ground in which we can grow the roots necessary to feed and sustain social action. I began to understand what Gandhi meant when he described prayer as "the most potent instrument of action."[1]

---

1   "Let Us Pray," no. 434 in *The Collected Works of Mahatma Gandhi*, vol. 83, January 20, 1946–April 13, 1945 (New Delhi : Publications Division, Ministry of Information and Broadcasting, Government of India, 1981), 372.

One could argue that meditation is the least active form of prayer possible. In silent, centering prayer, we sit quietly, waiting and still, yielded to the hidden work of God. A quiet, internal shift, a repeated return to the center as distractions attempt to pull us away, is the only perceptible activity. Centering prayer is deep listening. It has been described as "listening to the heartbeat of God."[2] What does this deliberate inaction have to do with Christ's call to active labor in the fields of God's kingdom (Matthew 9:37-38)?

Meditation offers tangible opportunities for us to

practice seeking first the kingdom of God. A brief period of meditation—even when filled with the usual distractions and temptations—offers an abundance of opportunities to claim and reclaim our allegiance to God. Fixing our eyes on Christ, we find

> Time spent with Jesus was the central identifying characteristic of a disciple and equipped the disciples to change the world. Why shouldn't the same be true for us?

a growing freedom from all other attractions. In fact, time spent with Jesus was the central identifying characteristic of a disciple and equipped the disciples to change the world. Why shouldn't the same be true for us? Dwelling with God equips us to respond to even the most pressing issues.

Meditation can prevent us from becoming desensitized

by torrents of bad news because it exposes us to the heartbeat of God. God's heart resonates with tender love for the entirety of creation, and in God's presence, our own hearts are made

---

2   See, among others, J. Philip Newell, *Listening for the Heartbeat of God: A Celtic Spirituality* (Mahwah, NJ: Paulist Press, 1997).

vulnerable and soft. Loved by God, we become attuned to the brokenness of our own lives and the world around us. We grieve with God and catch God's vision for the world as it might be. We begin to long for the kingdom of God to be made real, and that longing becomes a burning passion, a guiding light.

> Centered in the truth of our belovedness, we're freed to speak boldly and confidently in the face of entrenched perspectives.

Meditation addresses the overwhelming complexity

of the world's problems by steeping us in the creative reality of God's love. Centered in the truth of our belovedness, we're freed to speak boldly and confidently in the face of entrenched perspectives. Through the practice of saying no to all but Christ, we become people capable of looking at the problems around us without the hindrance of ego and personal gain. In meditation, we find the imagination, freedom, and confidence required to envision a path forward.

Meditation helps us determine what role is ours to

play by teaching us who we are. Resting in God's loving gaze, we confront the truth of our gifts and limitations and receive the invitation to accept ourselves as God accepts us, just as we are. Firmly positioned in truth and grace, we're uniquely situated to discern our own path—to find, as Frederick Buechner puts it, "the place where your deep gladness and the world's deep hunger meet."[3] In the midst of the many voices shouting for us to run here or go there, meditation tunes our hearts to the calm, quiet voice that says, "This is what I have made you for. This is who you are."

---

3   Frederick Buchner, *Wishful Thinking: A Seeker's ABC*, rev. ed. (San Francisco: HarperOne, 1993), 119.

Henri Nouwen describes the fruit of meditation in this way: "Securely rooted in personal intimacy with the source of life, it will be possible to remain flexible without being relativistic, convinced without being rigid, willing to confront without being offensive, gentle and forgiving without being soft, and true witnesses without being manipulative."[4]

Meditation offers a rudder to navigate our course of action as we respond to the call to live into the kingdom of God here and now in our everyday lives. Moving us deeper into the heart of God, meditation propels us and equips us to move deeper into the world as agents of redemption and reconciliation.

Talk about it

▶ What is your experience with prayer and social action? Do you see them as similar or oppositional expressions of Christian life?

▶ What struggles impede your life of action? Do you relate to my students' concerns of desensitization, lack of a clear path forward, and indecision about your own role in responding to injustice? Are there other concerns you would add to this list?

▶ What is your experience with meditation or centering prayer? Does framing prayer as a continual return to God's presence help clarify the aim of meditation?

▶ Try sitting quietly in God's presence. Set a timer (try starting with five to ten minutes), find a comfortable position, and offer your practice to God. Trust that your heartfelt intention to be with God is enough, no matter how much distraction or

4   Henri Nouwen, *In the Name of Jesus: Reflections on Christian Leadership* (New York: Crossroad, 1989), 31-32.

resistance you face. When you are done, spend a few minutes journaling or talking about the experience.

▶ Experiment with adding silent pauses into your day. Try returning to God for a brief moment whenever you find yourself overwhelmed or lacking direction.

▶ Prayer and action are two sides of the same coin. Which do you tend to focus on more: time with God or time in the world? What are the dangers or risks of focusing too much on one or the other?

About the Writer

Kelly Chripczuk is associate pastor at Grantham Brethren in Christ Church in Pennsylvania. She is also a spiritual director, writer, speaker, and adjunct professor in the biblical and religious studies department at Messiah College. Having received her training in spiritual direction through Oasis Ministries, Chripczuk offers contemplative retreat days and classes at local churches and retreat centers.

A graduate of Messiah College's biblical studies program, Chripczuk received her MDiv from Princeton Theological Seminary. Chripczuk writes regularly at www.thiscontemplativelife .org. She also offers a monthly newsletter called Quiet Lights. Her deep passion and delight is to awaken others to the reality of God's unwavering presence and love. Chripczuk lives with her husband and four children on the family's small farm in central Pennsylvania.

Discover all the books in the UPSIDE DOWN LIVING series

Identity and Aging

We get older every day, and as we age our lives change. In moving from youth to young adulthood, from middle-aged to retiree, we discover that life marches on even as our situations and identities continue to change. This study explores how we can age faithfully and gracefully, embracing ourselves through each phase of life.

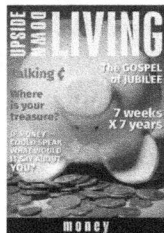

Money

Every day we face decisions that impact our wallets—and these decisions say a lot about our priorities. The way we use money can communicate power and strength, charity and selflessness. How does your use of money reflect or expand your faith? This study takes an honest look at financial choices and how we can view them through a lens of faith.

Parenting

Raising kids is hard enough. But raising kids to heed Jesus' upside-down call away from status and power and toward service and sharing? It can seem almost impossible. So how can parents model countercultural choices? What habits can help families joyfully follow Christ instead of the latest trend? Gather with your faith community to search the Scriptures and discuss how to raise faithful kids in the twenty-first century.

Prayer

Prayer can easily become an afterthought, a hasty sentence, a laundry list of all the things we want. But what if prayer is a time to find out what God wants for us—and for our world? What does it mean to pray that the kingdom would come here and now as it is in heaven? Explore these questions in this study, and learn prayer practices that nurture intimacy with God and sensitivity to God's dream for the world.

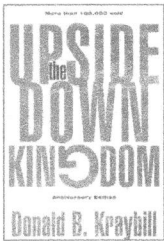

www.ingramcontent.com/pod-product-compliance
Lightning Source LLC
Chambersburg PA
CBHW031635040426
42452CB00007B/835